Laura Ingalls Wilder
~Pioneer Woman~

Dona Herweck Rice

Consultants

Vanessa Ann Gunther, Ph.D.
Department of History
Chapman University

Nicholas Baker, Ed.D.
Supervisor of Curriculum and Instruction
Colonial School District, DE

Katie Blomquist, Ed.S.
Fairfax County Public Schools

Publishing Credits

Rachelle Cracchiolo, M.S.Ed., *Publisher*
Conni Medina, M.A.Ed., *Managing Editor*
Emily R. Smith, M.A.Ed., *Series Developer*
Diana Kenney, M.A.Ed., NBCT, *Content Director*
Courtney Patterson, *Senior Graphic Designer*
Lynette Ordoñez, *Editor*

Image Credits: Cover and pp. 1, 17, 24 Granger, NYC; pp. 4 to 5 United States Capitol; p. 5 (top) John Schultz/ZUMA Press/Newscom , (bottom) NARA [299815]; p. 6 (left) Garth Williams estate/Harper Collins; pp. 6 (right), back cover Harper Collins; p.8 Danita Delimont/Getty Images; p. 9 Courtesy of Laura Ingalls Wilder Home Association Mansfield, MO; p. 11 (top) LOC [g4021e.ct003199]; pp. 11 to 12 Peter Newark American Pictures/Bridgeman Images; p. 12 (top) RMN-Grand Palais/Art Resource, NY, (bottom) Universal History Archive/UIG/Bridgeman Images; pp. 14, 18 Sarin Images/Granger, NYC; p. 14 (bottom) Harper Collins; image courtesy of Special Collections, Tutt Library, Colorado College, Colorado Springs, Colorado; p. 15 (top) Lyroky/Alamy Stock Photo, (bottom) Creative Commons maggiejp, used under CC BY-SA 2.0; p. 16 (front) Harper Collins, (back) South Dakota State Historical Society; pp. 19 (top left), 32 National Archives and Records Administration; p. 19 (top right) Herbert Hoover Presdential Library, (bottom) Laura Ingalls Wilder Memorial Society; p. 20 Living History Farms; p. 21 (top) Courtesy of Laura Ingalls Wilder Home Association Mansfield, MO, (bottom) Herbert Hoover Presidential Library, (left) UK Lutterworth Press; p. 22 Harper Collins; p. 23 Buddy Mays/Alamy Stock Photo; p. 24 Herbert Hoover Presdential Library; p. 25 Courtesy of Judy Green/Photographed by Beverly Kenworthy; p. 26 Bettmann/Getty Images; pp. 26, 27 American Library Assocation; p. 27 The State Historical Society of Missouri, Photograph Collection (C294_1); p. 31 John Schultz/ZUMA Press/Newscom; all other images from iStock and/or Shutterstock.

Library of Congress Cataloging-in-Publication Data

Names: Rice, Dona, author.
Title: Laura Ingalls Wilder : pioneer woman / Dona Herweck Rice.
Description: Huntington Beach, CA : Teacher Created Materials, 2017. | Includes index.
Identifiers: LCCN 2016034142 (print) | LCCN 2016048210 (ebook) | ISBN 9781493837984 (pbk.) | ISBN 9781480757639 (eBook)
Subjects: LCSH: Wilder, Laura Ingalls, 1867-1957--Juvenile literature. | Authors, American--20th century--Biography--Juvenile literature. | Women pioneers--United States--Biography--Juvenile literature.
Classification: LCC PS3545.I342 Z828 2017 (print) | LCC PS3545.I342 (ebook) |
  DDC 813/.52 [B] --dc23
LC record available at https://lccn.loc.gov/2016034142

Teacher Created Materials

5301 Oceanus Drive
Huntington Beach, CA 92649-1030
http://www.tcmpub.com

ISBN 978-1-4938-3798-4

Table of Contents

Go West!

"Go west!" they said.

The message was everywhere. In the general store, neighbors met and talked about it. Newspapers told of westward land available for the taking. A person only had to be bold enough to travel there and claim it. Farmers and townspeople feeling hemmed in and restricted by limited **resources** dreamed of wide-open spaces. They dreamed of a chance to own land. Families made plans through long winter months, looking toward the spring. That's when mountains and plains could be crossed by wagon or on foot.

"Go west!" the people heard. And go west they did.

Most travelers were men. They left to start new lives with opportunities once unknown to them. But, in growing numbers, women went as well. Women and children, young and old, they all **surged** westward. Many people sought a way to grab hold of the American dream!

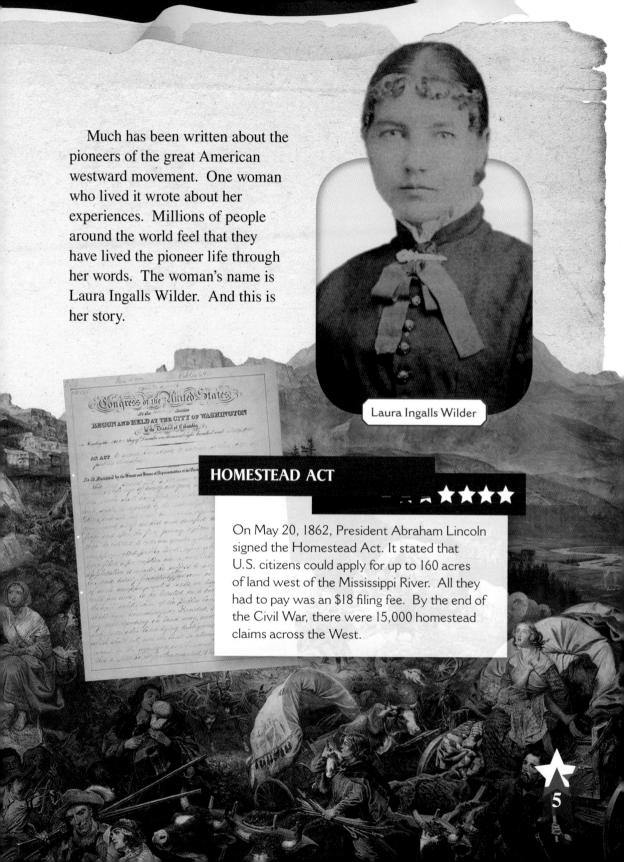

Much has been written about the pioneers of the great American westward movement. One woman who lived it wrote about her experiences. Millions of people around the world feel that they have lived the pioneer life through her words. The woman's name is Laura Ingalls Wilder. And this is her story.

Laura Ingalls Wilder

HOMESTEAD ACT

★★★★

On May 20, 1862, President Abraham Lincoln signed the Homestead Act. It stated that U.S. citizens could apply for up to 160 acres of land west of the Mississippi River. All they had to pay was an $18 filing fee. By the end of the Civil War, there were 15,000 homestead claims across the West.

Laura Ingalls

In 1869, a young girl named Laura sat at her father's knee. She listened to him tell wondrous stories of his childhood and life in the wilderness of Wisconsin, where the family lived. Pa, as Laura called him, told of meeting bears in the woods late at night. He told of runaway sleds and pigs. He told of the magic of watching a deer and her fawn in the moonlight.

Laura was enthralled by the stories and how her father told them. They would stay with her all her life. One day, she would use them to help write her first book, *Little House in the Big Woods*. The girl would grow up to be the famous and beloved author, Laura Ingalls Wilder. The book is a tribute to Laura's father, Charles Ingalls. It is also the beginning of a series of books that tell of the Ingalls family's pioneer life.

LITTLE HOUSE IN THE BIG WOODS

LAURA INGALLS WILDER

HELEN SEWELL
ERS ESTABLISHED 1817

This Garth Williams illustration from *Little House in the Big Woods* shows Pa, Ma, Laura, and Mary.

MA AND PA

★★★★★

Laura called her mother, whose name was Caroline, *Ma*. Today, most people do not use *Pa* and *Ma*, but many people still use *Grandpa* and *Grandma*.

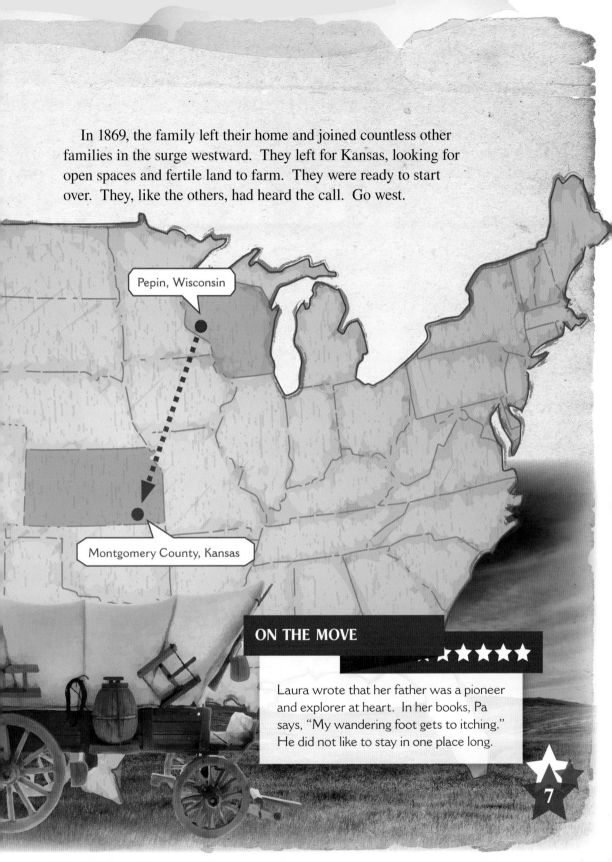

In 1869, the family left their home and joined countless other families in the surge westward. They left for Kansas, looking for open spaces and fertile land to farm. They were ready to start over. They, like the others, had heard the call. Go west.

Pepin, Wisconsin

Montgomery County, Kansas

ON THE MOVE

Laura wrote that her father was a pioneer and explorer at heart. In her books, Pa says, "My wandering foot gets to itching." He did not like to stay in one place long.

In the Beginning

Laura Elizabeth Ingalls was born on February 7, 1867, in a little log cabin. The cabin sat tucked into the woods near the town of Pepin, Wisconsin. Laura had one sister, Mary. Later, two more sisters—Carrie and Grace—were born. Their only brother, Freddie, died as a baby. Much of Laura's extended family lived near her. She played with her cousins. She enjoyed her grandma, grandpa, aunts, and uncles.

In time, the stories Pa shared began to change a bit. He talked about how many people were moving into the area. He told of the struggle to hunt due to the **scarcity** of wildlife. Pa told of the struggle to farm the wooded land. He began to talk about moving away.

A move to Kansas meant the family would leave the family circle. There would be no way to stay a part of one another's life. Letters mailed could take weeks or even months to arrive. The family wasn't sure they would ever see one another again.

Laura's parents knew that, to do the best for their family, they had to take the chance and move west.

replica of the Ingalls home near Pepin, Wisconsin

Pepin, Wisconsin, today

YOUR OWN BOOTSTRAPS

★★★★★★

Charles and Caroline Ingalls, Laura's parents, could "pull themselves up by their own bootstraps," as people said. They hunted and grew their own food. They made their own clothing. They even built their own house and furniture! There was little they couldn't do, and they taught their children to do the same.

"Indian Territory"

Charles and Caroline had read in the newspapers that land in Kansas was ready for U.S. **development**. This land, they thought, was open for the taking. They said goodbye to their parents and siblings. They sold their home and packed their wagon. They were ready to go.

Laura was just two when the family made this first move. They left for Kansas and a new life under its wide blue skies.

After several weeks riding in the wagon and camping along the way, they arrived in Montgomery County, Kansas. They found a **tract** of land on which to build their new home. Charles applied for a homestead. They built a house and planted a garden. This new place became their home.

What they didn't know—or perhaps ignored—is that the land already belonged to others. It was part of a wide area of land called the Osage Diminished Reserve. The Osage tribe had rights to the land. As Laura later described in her books, it was "Indian Territory." The Ingalls family had no right to settle there.

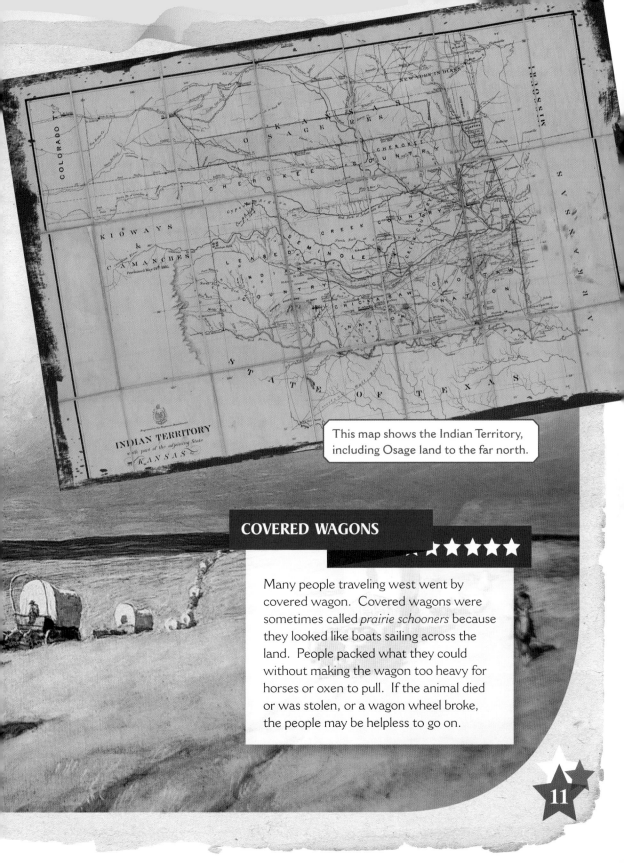

This map shows the Indian Territory, including Osage land to the far north.

COVERED WAGONS

Many people traveling west went by covered wagon. Covered wagons were sometimes called *prairie schooners* because they looked like boats sailing across the land. People packed what they could without making the wagon too heavy for horses or oxen to pull. If the animal died or was stolen, or a wagon wheel broke, the people may be helpless to go on.

Tensions between the settlers and the Osage were high. In her book, *Little House on the Prairie*, Laura recounts the allure of a **culture** she didn't know. She was drawn to the glimpses she saw and fragments she heard about Osage life. With Pa, Laura visited former Osage camps to see what she could learn. She was eager to know more.

Laura also tells of the fear some of her family and other settlers had. They could not understand any hostility the Osage people felt toward them. They believed they were in the right and that the Osage should move. The Osage, of course, resented the settlers living on their land. It was theirs by history and by law.

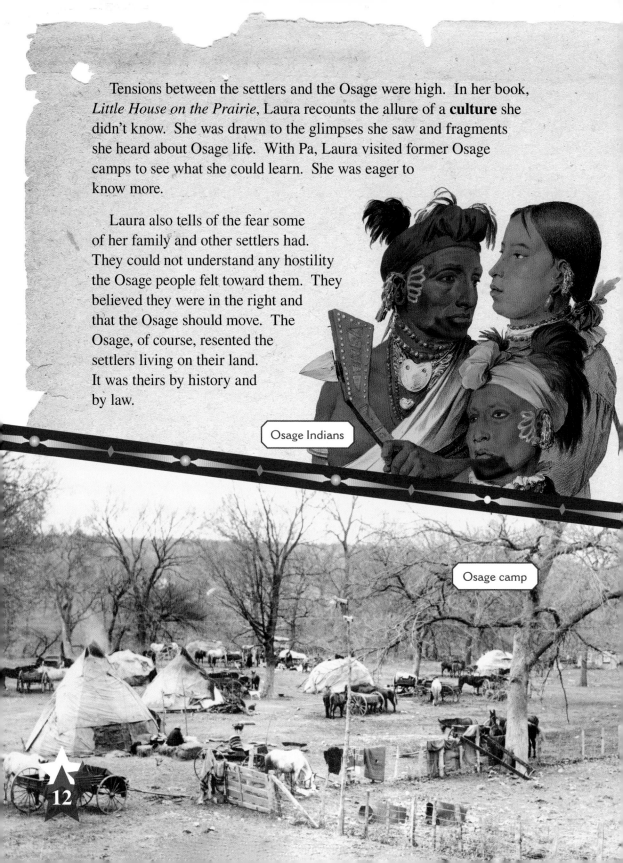

Osage Indians

Osage camp

12

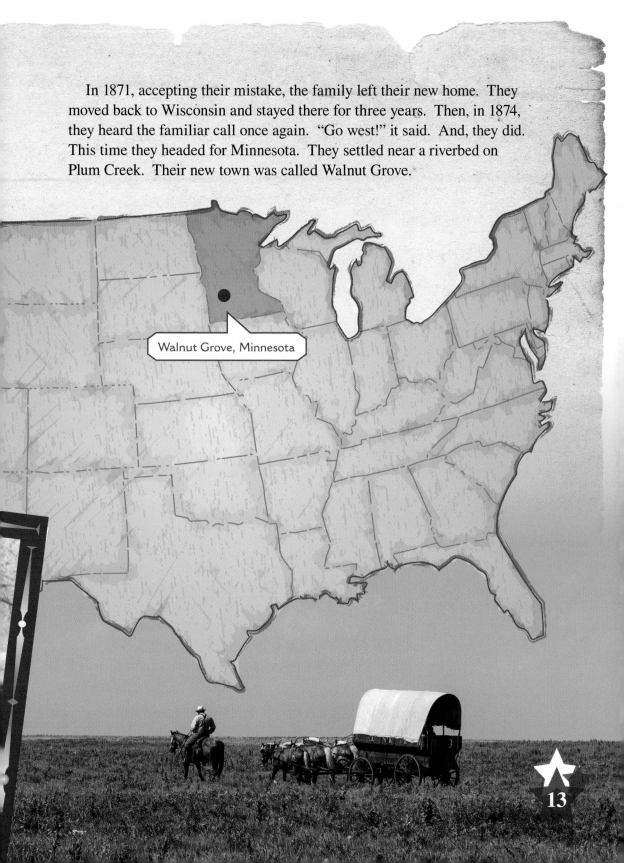

In 1871, accepting their mistake, the family left their new home. They moved back to Wisconsin and stayed there for three years. Then, in 1874, they heard the familiar call once again. "Go west!" it said. And, they did. This time they headed for Minnesota. They settled near a riverbed on Plum Creek. Their new town was called Walnut Grove.

Walnut Grove, Minnesota

Reaching for the Dream

The Ingalls family felt hopeful about their new home. The land seemed rich. The town was on the rise, and the family enjoyed new friendships. They built a house and planted crops. They helped to build the local church. The girls went to school, which their pioneer life did not always allow.

But success was beyond the family's reach. During the 1870s, Minnesota suffered a series of grasshopper **plagues**. The flying, hopping insects covered the land in the millions. They ate all the crops. They stripped leaves from trees and grass from fields. The Ingalls crop was lost two years in a row. The family was deep in **debt** and had little **income**.

Farmers attempt to save their crops from grasshoppers.

ON THE BANKS OF PLUM CREEK
LAURA INGALLS WILDER

LIFE IN MINNESOTA

★★★★★

A fictionalized version of the Walnut Grove, Minnesota, years of Laura's life is told in her book, *On the Banks of Plum Creek*.

Masters Hotel today in Burr Oak, Iowa

Luck turned when they were given an opportunity in Burr Oak, Iowa. Charles and Caroline would manage the Masters Hotel, a friend's business. In 1876, the family loaded the wagon. Iowa would be their new home. But, tragedy found them again. Freddie, the Ingalls's only son, died at less than 10 months of age. The family was heartbroken.

DUGOUT

★★★

The first house the Ingalls family had in Walnut Grove was a home made by digging into a hillside and adding a wooden front door. It was called a *dugout house*. This is a replica.

15

Life in Iowa was strange for Laura and her sisters. Freddie's death was deeply sad for them all. There was also a strange encounter with a wealthy local woman. The woman tried to adopt Laura away from her family! The woman was shocked that Pa and Ma would not give up their daughter. She was sure that they would want Laura to have the opportunities she could provide. Laura's parents were horrified, of course. They turned her down.

Perhaps these sad and strange experiences are the reasons that Iowa is the only part of her story that Laura does not share in her books.

Mary, Grace, Charles, Laura, Carrie, and Caroline (from left to right)

The family's last days in Walnut Grove are told at the beginning of *By the Shores of Silver Lake*.

By the Author of LITTLE HOUSE IN THE BIG WOODS

BY THE SHORES of SILVER LAKE

LAURA INGALLS WILDER

The Ingalls family returned to Walnut Grove after just two years away. Again, they struggled to survive. And then, tragedy returned. Laura's sister, Mary, became very ill and nearly died. She survived the illness, but her sight did not. Mary was left blind.

Saddened and worn out, the family was **bereft**. They had to find a new life. That's when opportunity came to their door once again.

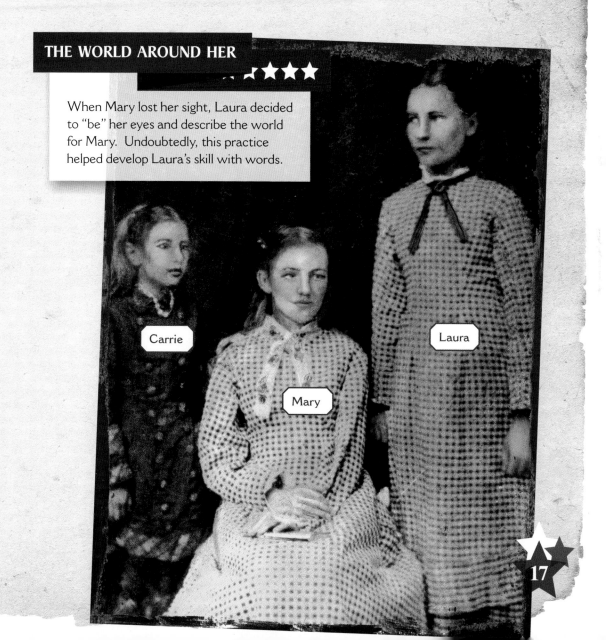

THE WORLD AROUND HER

★★★★

When Mary lost her sight, Laura decided to "be" her eyes and describe the world for Mary. Undoubtedly, this practice helped develop Laura's skill with words.

Carrie

Laura

Mary

On Their Own

Charles was offered a job with the railroads. At the time, tracks were being laid across the country. For the first time, people could travel quickly between east and west. Charles would be the timekeeper and storekeeper for the workers laying the tracks.

A crew builds a railroad in the Dakota territory in 1879.

In 1879, the family moved with the railroad. Charles earned the money they needed to start their new life. The town of De Smet was being established in the Dakota Territory. (Later, the territory would become the states of North and South Dakota.) The railroad went past De Smet. There, the Ingalls family stayed. They were among the town's first residents. They also filed a homestead claim. They planted cottonwood trees around their new house. Those trees grow even today.

That same year, a young man named Almanzo Wilder left his family and filed a claim near De Smet. He would play a big part in Laura's future.

Charles Ingalls's homestead application

Almanzo Wilder, whose childhood is told in Laura's book, *Farmer Boy*

De Smet

Laura worked hard to support the family homestead. She worked side by side with her father in the fields and her mother in the house. She also became a schoolteacher at the age of 15! She was active and **industrious**. She caught the eye of Almanzo, and he caught hers. When Laura was 18, the two wed. They moved to Almanzo's claim.

replica of the Bouchie School, where Laura taught at 15

TEACHER

★★★★★★★★

To become a teacher in the 1800s in the United States, a person had to pass a test of knowledge in different subject areas. Most teachers were between 16 and 25 years old. Women usually quit when they married.

The early years of their marriage were among the hardest Laura had ever known. Except for the birth of their daughter, Rose, in 1886, tragedy was around every corner. In 1888, Laura and Almanzo became deathly ill with **diphtheria** (dif-THEER-ee-eh). Almanzo went back to work too soon and suffered a **stroke**. He was left with crippled feet. That same year, the couple had a son, but the baby soon died. One year later, their home burned to the ground. Years of drought and a barn fire left them penniless and in debt.

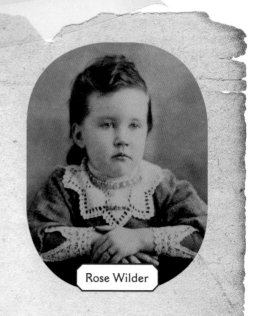

Rose Wilder

The family moved to Florida for Almanzo's health. But, they returned to De Smet in 1892. They rented a small house and worked to save every penny they could. They had made up their minds. They were going to move one last time. They had heard the pioneer call once again.

Four books in Laura's series tell about her life as a young adult, including "the first four years" of her married life.

Laura and Almanzo during their time in Florida

The Wilders managed to save $100. They tucked the money into a writing desk Almanzo had made for Laura. Then, they set out in a wagon of their own in the summer of 1894. They were headed for the Missouri Ozarks and a new life. Laura kept a diary of the long journey. The diary was published years later as the book *On the Way Home*.

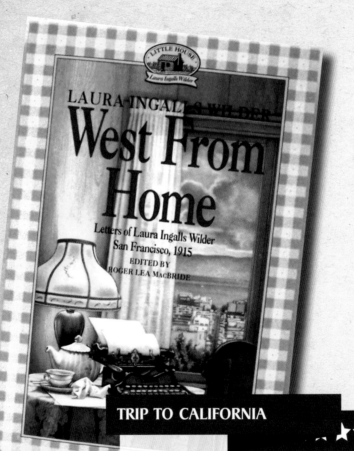

TRIP TO CALIFORNIA ★★★

Laura visited Rose in 1915 in California. While there, she wrote many letters home to Almanzo. The letters were later published in the book *West from Home*.

Rocky Ridge Farm

On August 31, they arrived in Mansfield, Missouri. After a scare in which they thought they'd lost the money, they placed it as a down payment on 40 acres of rocky farmland. They named the place Rocky Ridge Farm. It would be their home for the rest of their long lives. As an adult, Rose would one day live as far west as California. But Laura had found her final home at last.

Laura and Almanzo built their new house themselves. They used materials from their farm. It took them many years, and they had many setbacks. But, they **persevered**.

A Dream Achieved

The work was long and hard. But, step by step, things got better for the Wilders. Rose thrived in school. She grew up to become a respected writer. She traveled the world and led a life that Laura never dreamed was possible. The Wilders became successful farmers. In fact, they were renowned for their farming skills.

Rose Wilder's graduation photo

Laura in 1917

In 1912, Laura was asked to write for a local paper. She wrote a column about farm life called "As a Farm Woman Thinks." In 1919, an article she wrote was printed in a national magazine. In 1925, one more article was published. These were just the start of her writing career. With Rose's support, Laura wrote about her life as a pioneer. She wrote with vivid detail so that readers felt as though they were pioneers themselves. In 1932, Harper Brothers published the first of Laura's books. *Little House in the Big Woods* was a huge success! Fans begged for more.

Mansfield, Missouri
Dec. 20th, 1949

Dear Mrs. Spear,
Your letter of Dec. 4. has just now reached me.
I am returning your check because I can not send you the book. You can likely get it at a book store. If not you can order it directly from the publisher, Harper + Brothers, 49 E. 33d. St. New York—16 N.Y.
I am enclosing my autograph for you to paste in the book. It is much easier than to send the book.
Your letter is very interesting

FAN MAIL

Laura received countless letters from fans asking about her life. People traveled from miles around to visit her on Rocky Ridge Farm.

Pioneer to Author

Laura gave them more! She published eight books from 1932 to 1943. Each retold part of her story from Pepin to De Smet. What Laura came to see was that her story was, in many ways, the story of the United States. She traveled the paths the country traveled as it grew and changed through the 1800s. Laura saw the country grow. In fact, she helped it grow. She planted roots of her own and left her mark. And she left a **legacy** for future generations.

Laura Ingalls Wilder autographs a book.

HONORED ★★★★★

The Laura Ingalls Wilder Award was established in 1954 to honor authors and illustrators who have made lasting contributions to children's literature across many years. Laura was the first recipient.

Laura and Almanzo in the 1940s

Laura and Almanzo lived long, full lives. Each died at Rocky Ridge Farm. Almanzo died in 1949. Laura died in 1957, three days after her 90th birthday.

Laura's many fans still visit the farm. In fact, they visit all her home sites. They often follow the pioneer path she followed. They want to see what Laura saw. Through her writing, they, too, hear the pioneer call. They want to experience it for themselves…and they *can*, through Laura's eyes.

NEWBERY HONOR BOOKS

★★★★

The Newbery Honor is among the highest awards for children's literature. Five of the Little House books received this award.

FOR THE MOST DISTINGUISHED CONTRIBUTION TO AMERICAN LITERATURE FOR CHILDREN

Sing It!

"Oh! Susanna" was written by Stephen Foster and published in 1848. It is an American folk song that Laura and her family knew well. Charles Ingalls often played his fiddle for the family, and Mary learned to play the piano. The whole family sang together. This is one of the many songs they enjoyed playing and singing.

Oh! Susanna

By Stephen Foster

I come from Alabama with my banjo on my knee.
I'm going to Louisiana, my true love for to see.
It rained all night the day I left, the weather it was dry.
The sun so hot I froze to death, Susanna, don't you cry.

Chorus:
Oh! Susanna, Oh don't you cry for me,
For I come from Alabama with my banjo on my knee.

I had a dream the other night, when everything was still;
I thought I saw Susanna dear, a coming down the hill.
A buckwheat cake was in her mouth, a tear was in her eye,
Says I, I'm coming from the south, Susanna, don't you cry.

Chorus

I soon will be in New Orleans, and then I'll look around,
And when I find Susanna, I'll fall upon the ground.
But if I do not find her, then I will surely die,
And when I'm dead and buried, Oh, Susanna, don't you cry.

Glossary

bereft—deeply sad because of a death or tragic outcome that feels like a death

culture—the beliefs and ways of a group of people

debt—an amount of money owed to someone

development—the act or process of creating or growing something over a period of time

diphtheria—a disease caused by a bacterial infection that makes breathing difficult and can be deadly

income—money earned from work or investments

industrious—hard working

legacy—something that happened or that comes from someone in the past

persevered—continued doing something even in the face of great difficulty

plagues—large numbers of harmful or destructive things

resources—supplies

scarcity—a small supply of something

stroke—a serious illness caused when a blood vessel in the brain becomes blocked or broken, often resulting in paralysis or death

surged—pushed ahead

tract—an area of land

Index

Your Turn!

Life on the Homestead

Charles Ingalls "proved up" on his homestead on May 11, 1886. He finally owned the land. Knowing what you know of Laura's life, imagine you are a homesteader in the 1800s. What do you do all day? Do you have help? Are you lonely? Are you hopeful or discouraged? Write a journal entry about a day in your life on the homestead.